Wild
Plums

Poems

D1304769

JOHN HERM

Printed by Recondier Press 2018

Book design and cover by
Mari Anderson

Photographs by
Hunter Connors Herm

In Memory of Eugene Field (1850-1895)

CONTENTS

ONE

Mother's Garden	1
The Hummingbird	2
Arbor Day	3
Wild Plums	5
Slow Spring	7
October Grass	8
Prairie Seas	9
Murder Up Ahead	10
Climbing Tree	11
The Last Morel	12
Monarchs	14
The Dyreson Bridge	15
Sandhill Gates	16
The Ice Shoe	17
Nighthawks	19

TWO

Ma's A' Waitin'	21
Movin' Slow	23
Come Thanksgivin'	26
Christmas Comin'	28
Reg'lar Times	30
Raising Days	32
Grandpa's Anvil	35

THREE

Sandhills	37
The Father in Me	38

"Ol Hick'ry   40
The Night Marauder   42
Kingfisher   43
The Big Burr Oak   44
Barn Swallows   46
Drought   48
Sweet Dreams   49
Good News   51
Winter Wheat   53
Buzzards   55
Winter Wood   56
Flowing Waters   57
Snowtrap   58
Lighthouse Keeper   59
Henry's Ghost   60
Maine   61
Iceland   62
Theresa   63
Facing East   64

FOUR

Sip of Gin   67
The Window   69
Slow 'er on Down   70
Shelves   71
The Closet   73
Gone Girl   74
Always on Sunday   75
The Party   78
Time   80
The River   81

Part
1

Mother's Garden

I pick through rock piles others made
on sides of fields now deep in shade
so I can find some stepping stones
and build a path to ease the grade

in Mother's Garden ... full of mist
that she had sown with seeds she'd kissed.
Deep rooted now, full glory grown ...
there I'll lay my stepping stones.

I hear her voice, her favorite place
where flowers bloom in quiet grace ...
She spoke of gardens I might make
with stepping stones to ease the grade.

The Hummingbird

The other day when I was reading on the porch,
I heard a tiny tap on the window
and thought nothing of it
until I looked about on the ground outside
and there he was … lying under the window.

A hummingbird who had been flying by was fooled by
the glass,
misjudged his course and crashed, … probably
headfirst.

I picked him up with my right hand
and gently placed him in my left.
I felt I was holding nearly nothing
but there he was …
Such color in his ruby throat,
so shiny green his wings …

I watched his stillness … hoping hard
he wouldn't die in my hand of all places.

And he didn't.
He recovered in a few minutes
and off he buzzed … quick as a dragonfly…
to places I have never been or will ever know.

Arbor Day

If I could be a tree
I'd like to be
an Oak.
I would stand sturdy in storms,
not willow or billow, bend or break.
No one could see the winter wind.

Maybe I'd be a Pear tree
with brilliant white spring blossoms
and grow perfect pears
that ripen slowly in the cellar
for tarts at Christmas.

Perhaps a shag bark Hickory
and I'd grow the tastiest nut of all
to crumble on cake frostings,
better yet with chocolate on ice cream.

I'd also like to be a Maple,
the hardest wood of all,
and turn golden red in October,
then share my spring sweet water
for syrup and candy in March.

I could be a Pine, a Cherry
an Ash an Elm or a Walnut.
A Mulberry, an Apple, a Peach or Plum,
a Poplar, a Cottonwood
with fluttering leaves in a gentle wind.

As a tree
I'd be
fire of winter warmth
and cooling summer shades,
holding banks and grades,
as my roots run deep
for long winter sleep.

If I were a tree
I could be
a beautiful blanket chest,
a tall handsome wardrobe,
maybe a long wide harvest table
and everyone would touch me every day
while I listen to laughter
in the house I helped build.

But I can't be a tree,
only dream to be
with birds in my arms
who sing perfect songs.

Wild Plums

It's February
and I'm spreading some
Wild Plum jam
on whole wheat bread
Mother taught me to bake.

The jam reminds me
of the color of wild plums
on the inside …
and on the outside.

I remember they were the very first fruit
to flower last spring after the snow melt.
The trees are low
with snaggly branches
hugging the ground … hiding,
so even country folk assume
they're some sort of bush
where rabbits live
and pay them no mind.

Most times the plums are gnarled
from a strong fungus I think,
but this year the plums were perfect
and we all picked as many as we could and made
Wild Plum jam.

The jam preserves the wild taste
from the effort of the golden flesh
that clings so hard to the stone
to orchard more purple plums …

It's breakfast in February
and I feel rich that I search
for hidden fruit in secret places.

Slow Spring

Do you remember the year of the slowest Spring?
When the grass stayed brown and wouldn't green
and the bluebirds came but wouldn't sing.

The trees held buds but nary a leaf,
and the flowers lay still in the ground beneath
from the frost that came most ev'ry night,
though the sun shone clear and crisp and bright.

And all of us thought she'd never show,
we watched and we waited through dustings of snow…

Sometime in May, Spring finally came,
and things seemed back to nearly the same.

For then all the birds sang the purest of notes
and the bluebells flourished 'neath the great oaks,
the greens from the garden so tender and nice
tasted even better with watercress spice.

The daffodils bloomed their prettiest ever,
the scilla so blue and lasted forever …
The asparagus sprigs … had the best flavor
and that rhubarb pie … we'd just sit … and savor.

Do you remember the year of the slowest Spring?
With the best of things it came to bring.
Let's welcome Slow Spring (for always she'll grow)
to temper our patience of the world that we know.

October Grass

In October
something happens to the grass.
The leaves thicken in the fall sun
and slowly turn a vibrant deep green.

I think it's because of the flourish
before November wilt,
like birds who fatten before the trip,
or when minds suddenly focus
before a long winters' rest,
alert and ready
if there may be no spring.

Every year
I'm more aware of the greening grass
under the brilliant blue sky
amid the red golden browns of October.

Prairie Seas

Not long ago
these glaciered plains
held maize and buffalo …
and when the collared horse arrived
the endless prairies slowly died
from furrowed fields of cultured crops,
savannah oaks were felled and chopped.
Today we mostly drive on by
the ground where buried prairies lie.
But some folks now have sown the soil
a brave and visioned few,
back to lands of long ago
where hardy plants in splendor grow.
Seeds were resting from centuries passed
with native strength they did outlast
the years of plow and harrow tills
with sturdy roots and patience still …
for every year some new arise,
kindled by the sweeping fires.
It's in our veins
these flowing plains
where flowers bloom among the grains.
Rustling winds have beckoned me
to aimless wander on most my days
and slip into the prairie sea …
deep in birdsfoot purple sheen.
I pause for handsome birds who sing …
then startled by the pheasant wing.
My mind floats free to times ago …
I hear the hooves of buffalo …
I feel some spirits walk with me …
We drift away on prairie seas …

Murder Up Ahead

On the road
hunkered in black …

Spying my car
before I spot them.

They wait for me …
watching me.

I know them
yet I don't really.

They know me though …
They are the Crows …

Feasting on the dead
ever wary lest they be …

They appear as one
until they burst apart …

Their timing always perfect.
It's a trio again …

Screaming throaty caws
and flapping hard their awkward wings
into the haunting sky
that Van Gogh painted.

Climbing Tree

I was raised in the farmhouse
my great grandfather built
where there is still a gigantic oak in the front yard
us four kids climbed most every day.

My brother would boost me up
until I was tall enough to reach myself,
then we'd walk around the strong thick limbs,
stepping safe in sturdiness among the robins.

My dad said the tree
was born three of four hundred years ago
with a long healed scar on its five-foot belly
from being a hitching post when great Grandpa
was a kid.

There is also a deep hole in the trunk
Dad and his brother made
from hatchet throwing contests when they were kids.
I'd stick my hand in there if I felt brave.

We spent hours in the comfort of those limbs,
scooching away from the trunk when we dared.
The tree taught us balance for we never fell
from the cavern coolness of summer shade.

We'd no idea of its ancient beckon
as we were tree dwellers long ago.
It's in our blood, climbing up,
lofting in limbs above danger below.

Toward the north was a tall rope swing
with a wide wooden seat
where you could stand up
and fly high if you pumped your arms.

We were kids and full of dreams,
we were kids without a care,
that was way back then
and that alluring oak's still standing there.

So I often think of that grand ol' tree,
all the things it means to me,
the years we kids all had
growing along with that climbing tree.

The Last Morel

Every year or so near the end of May
I have to face the saddening day
of a bittersweet dinner I have to tell
when it's time to eat the last morel.

For two or three weeks I've daily dined,
but today's the day I feel it's time
to open the fridge (with half a pout)
to grab the last few… am I really out?

I've hid 'em from friends who wanted to know
if I'd found a bunch where they usually grow,
(I had 'em for breakfast 'n dinner too…)
I've had second helpings when I should'a been
through.

Some years they're rare as four-leaf clovers,
but it's always tough when the season's over.
Oh my, how they cast their magic spell…
yet today's the day for the last morel!

I'll fry 'em up good to stretch 'em on out
since it'll be 'nother year (there's nary a doubt)
'til I get to taste that nutty flavor,
but there's still these left for me to savor.

I take extra care to stir and sauté
so they're cooked just perfect this special day.
My tongue always lingers and a tear starts to well …,
it's so hard to swallow … this one last morel.

Monarchs

When I glanced at the concrete resting pad by my garage,
I noticed a beautiful monarch butterfly taking a break,
slowly moving its wings back and forth …
But there was something odd about the monarch,
so I walked over and looked closer.
There were actually two monarchs,
their bodies locked, appearing as one.
Just as I bent over a bit
off they flew … wings struggling in dangerous
herky-jerky flight.
It appeared they might tumble out of the sky and crash
but they landed in the closest tree to rest.
I watched them flit from one branch to another
for quite awhile.
I knew they'd soon be on their way through Texas to Mexico.
I read later it would be their last flight.

The monarchs somehow reminded me
when my wife and I hugged each other the whole journey
on that long trip south to Illinois
to see my dying mother one last time.

The Dyreson Bridge

We come upon this river's bend,
the quiet current churning,
these banks are strong and gently send
water on endless journey.
Storms deluge a rising stream
can birth a swift impasse.
A safer crossing bred this dream
and wrought this span to last.
This low truss bridge has joined the path
with girder steel design,
its wooden planks shall let us pass
one carriage at a time.
The Bridge built here ... brings neighbors near ...
no further need ... to ford the stream ...

This poem was written for the dedication of the restoration of an 1890's bridge in the Town of Dunn.

Sandhill Gates

These graceful gates … arching high
where Sandhills soar … through sunrise skies.

They proudly speak a long held dream
of roots grown deep where neighbors meet.
Sturdy monuments of steel and stone
hallow this ground for time unknown.

Headstones mark those sleeping here,
their passing voices echo clear
of chaptered stories on prairie seas …
they chose this land just as we …

We all shall fly on Sandhill wings …
and return to rest … in eternal spring.

*This poem was written for the dedication of majestic
wrought-iron gates with life-sized Sandhill cranes at the
entry to the Town of Dunn cemetery.*

The Ice Shoe

I happened upon this abandoned farm
and walked the land with all its charm.
I wondered who'd left this special place
whose prairie blooms a color'd embrace.

The house fallen down but sat by a creek,
up high enough so rains wouldn't seep.
The yard was choked with weeds that swayed
where once some children laughed and played.

I rebuilt the house with one of my own
'n fixed the barns where stock once roamed
this wavy land with the rappling creek
so peaceful here … I needn't speak.

'N while I toiled 'n kept a doin'
I kept my eye on a field stone ruin
with crumbled mortar but upright still
and squarely dug in the side of the hill.
I wasn't sure what once took place
within these walls that made this space.

But soon came the days to restore these walls
for they held but storied waste and all.
And while I rummaged 'n looked for clues
well … right there it was … a horse's shoe!

The shoe was weathered with worn down cleats
that once gave purchase on icy sheets
to pull his ice-block laden sled
from the frozen lake to this ice-house shed.

And I think how hard it must have been
when things were done by horse back then.
They sawed and cut the ice in blocks
to cool and save their cherished crops.

I love to picture that tall strong horse
who wore this shoe and stayed his course
to where I stand in this quilt of stone
by the singing creek that no one owns.

Nighthawks

When the Queen Ann's Lace was folded brown
And the sedums burst their purple crown,
The dusk was turning a cloudy sky
When up came a neighbor stopping by.

Soon I knew such reason why
Some stripe'd wings were flashing bright
Oh! The joy of it all … in the crisp air fall
At the stunning sight of a Nighthawk flight.

The squadrons banked and swerved and dived,
The bluegrass prairie had come alive,
We marveled amidst the acrobat throng,
Their mouths agape in silent song.

We ducked our heads from darting swoops,
we wondered what had flocked the group…
They must be headed south somewhere
bolstered by them feasting there.

The following days I hoped they'd show
but they had come to whither go …

I shan't forget so rare a night,
I dream them now in dusky light,
our quiet world in surreal surprise,
that mystic time when the Nighthawks fly.

Part
2

Ma's A' Waitin'

Purty long winter with all that snow,
one day in Januar' twas forty b'low,
but today I saw a crocus comin',
see Spring is here 'n things 'r hummin'.

The sun shoots up a whole lot early
'n folks after church seem quite 'n a hurry.
Now Ma's a'waitin' fer lilacs ta bloom
while I'm a hopin' school's out soon.

Pa's gittin' ready ta plow w'th the team
'n Gram's a' givin' the house a clean.
Big Sister Anne's bin winkin' at boys
'n no longer plays with silly ol' toys.

Ain't near warm ta move the stove
but the wood pile's gone by the hick'ry grove.
Now I'm jist achin' ta be outside
'n hop my coaster fer a good long ride.

Frost is outa the winter ground
'n hawgs 'r laughin' 'n rootin' around.
Calves 'r prancin' 'n kick their heels,
mother cow acts like it's no big deal.

Them crazy chickens don't ever rest
a' scratchin' 'round ta make a nest.
Coons 'r out 'n 'possum too,
flop-eared dawgs 'a sniffin' the dew.

Grouse 'r thumpin' all day long
while blackbirds sing that whirrin' song.
Robins 'r whistlin' through air that's wet,
there's cruisin' ducks with wings all set.

Now Chubby—he's a 'diggin' fer worms
showed some t'the girls ta watch 'em squirm.
Chubby 'n me bin checkin' the crick
a'sneakin ' round trout with willow sticks.
'N we laugh 'n holler 'til the sun goes down
'n git up real early without a sound.

Now Spring she wonders me jist how she grows,
preacherman says only God knows.
Boy, I sure am glad she's here agin,
folks all askin' jist where she's bin.
Chubby 'n me'll be fishin' soon
while Ma's a'waitin' that lilac perfume.

Movin' Slow

Seems spring's jist here w'all its thunder,
but Ma now sez, we slipped into summer.
I'm tryin' ta figur' the day it came,
late spring 'n summer, they seem the same.

The birds bin singin' way fore dawn,
when the sun gits up, b'gosh they're gone.
Gram's up stirrin' that blackberry jelly,
'n Sports's diggin' holes ta cool his belly.

Ma cooks lite with barely a fire,
'n Pa goes weedin', but gits real tired.
I start chorin' 'n soon I'm sweaty,
Gramps keeps sayin' that air's too heavy.

The heat blurs off the big barn roof,
horses jist stand 'n lift a back hoof.
The beef bunch up 'neath the wide oak tree...
seems everythin's frozen with all this heat.

Hawgs're sleepin' all caked with mud,
ol' Boss jist lays 'n rolls 'er cud.
We're all movin' slow 'neath this white hot sky,
seems only thing alive'z these no-good flies.

A bumble buzzes by 'n I stand rock-still,
he stares me down jist' ta check my will,
but I fooled 'im through 'n back slowly away,
then run real hard 'n go hide in the hay.

I should be chorin', I sure know that,
'fore I do, I takin' a nap,
right here in the grass to watch the clouds,
make scary critters a'driftin' 'round…
I close my eyes, but she's 'lil too bright,
'n kick off my boots… they're feelin' tight.

Jist I git dreamin' in that wide still sky,
a Red-tail screams that piercin' cry,
I know he spies me from way up high,
(he makes me shiver … I ain't sure why),
He rarely flaps 'n glides on 'n on,
he screams once more … 'n then he's gone.

She's steamin' now 'n we go soak in the creek,
jist one o'these days seems a winters' week.
Then 'round comes evenin' w'that sky deep blue,
but Pa keeps sayin' there's more to do.

Soon the sun's all through, but t'ain't over yet,
we go git fireflies with hands fer nets.
The crickets're screechin' that scratchy noise,
we hide 'n seek … girls agin' boys.

'N while I'm hunkered in the black night air,
a big-eared owl hoots me a scare.
He hackled my neck 'n I thought I was chillin'!,
but I settled right down from tha' soft Whip-'r-willin'.

Soon we git tuckered 'n go off to bed,
but Gram's still up, fannin' her head,
Gramps is up too 'n sez with a cough,
he's hopin' a storm'll cool us off.

24

Me, I'm layin' here jist thinkin' on
what makes these sweltered days so long …
I vision that day I kin smell the fall,
(I reckon my favorit' time of all).
'N I near-forgit winter with 'er shiverin' snows,
since we slipped into summer 'n we're all movin' slow.

Come Thanksgivin'

The trees 'r all bare 'n days gittin' short
'n Pa's bin huntin' with birddawg Sport
while I'm in school a'drawin' on slate,
but tommora's Thanksgivin' 'n I can't wait.

The teacher hollers one more song ta sing,
I figur' ta be gone 'fore the bell rings
'n run all the way home down the gravel road
as fast as I kin 'cause it's purty cold.

Now I ain't sure jist what it is
w' all these here folks called relativ's
who keep on talkin' 'bout turkey 'n trimmin's
'n how they eat like hawgs come Thanksivin'.

The fellers tell stories all nite 'bout deer
(the'z all drinkin' whiskey 'n homemade beer).
They keep laughin' a'loud Ma started shishin'
'n I sneak downstairs w' both ears a' listnin'.

Then the fellers git ready way 'fore dawn
'n Ma fries eggs w' a great big yawn.
They stumble out the door 'n Sport gives a whine
all kinda glassy eyed w' bucks on their mind.
When I git up the kitchen's ablaze
with ladies all jabberin' in some sorta craze,
they each got their job or special dish
but me, I'm makin' a Thanksgivin' wish.

I hope my Pa he shoots a deer
n' wish cousin Bob'd soon git here
cause I'm tired a' playin' w' sister Anne,
she'd ruther help Ma stir fryin' pans.

Now Pa 'n the men, they got those bucks,
they all kept sayin' it was some kinda luck.
They strung 'em up high in the old oak tree,
I guess for all the ladies ta see.

Then we si'down for dinner after a real quick rest,
there's so much food the table's a mess.
Pa says grace 'n we close our eyes
('cept me I'm a 'sniffin' that pun'kin pie).
Then we grab the bowls w' all kinds o' taters,
there's berries 'n breads 'n even t'maters.

It's all so good, food keeps a' passin'
'n 'fore too long my belt won't fassen,
my belly starts achin' 'n my heads a swimmin',
y'see, I eat like a hawg come Thanksgivin'.

Christmas Comin'

We pass'd Thanksgivin' a while ago
'n things'r quiet with all this snow.
The ducks took off jist last week
'cause ice is reachin' across the creek.
Tha' Nor'easter keeps the windmill hummin'
but I don't mind … 'cause Chrismas comin'!
The cousins'll come 'n we'll all go sleddin',
they ain't been 'round since tha' hot summer weddin'.
We'll use the ridge with all the bumps
'n Danny'll steer so we miss the stumps.
Now Gramma smiles 'n forgits ta scold,
Grandpa's mutterin' his feets is cold.
Even big sis Annie'll take a tease
while Ma fries cakes with a 'lil more grease.
Pa's a 'worried we got 'nuff meats,
'n still he flips the dawgs a piece.
The critters 'r sleepin' down their dens,
'n eggs come slow from under the hens.
Cats hunker down ta cover their paws
while Sport snuffs snow 'n snaps 'is jaws.
The hawgs've quit their summer squealin'
cattle stand 'round … with frosty breathin'.
The horses seem shaggy all'va sudden,
it's like ever'ones ready… fer Christmas comin'.
I jist spied a fox who's on the snoop
a' slinkin' right towards our chicken coop,
so Sport 'n me, we run 'im off good
'lickety-split he hightail't the woods.
Come evenin' time, we all huddle in

'n fill the stove from the hick'ry bin.
We down big dinners with all the trimmin's,
(I'm countin' the days we pass'd Thanksgivin').
Then right 'fore bed, Pa gits tha' notion
to chase me 'round in a big commotion.
He keeps on teasin' "you need a good lickin'"
but I fly too quick to my ... feathertickin'.
'n then I'm lyin' there all alone
wondrin' if I care to really know

if Ma was true or was she funnin'
"The times'r best ... when Christmas comin'."

Reg'lar Times

I got onta thinkin' jist yesterday
what makes my life so often gay,
'n on my list it clearly show'd
why it's those darn good neighbors down the road.

Our times seem hurried 'n fill'd w' 'biz
'n folks don't know what neighbor is
but if wife 'n I want ta stretch the day,
we call t'the neighbors straight away.

It's pure good fun us gittin' t'gether
'n the food we share seems 'lil better.
We relish the times like sugar'd candy
sides all that, they're doggone handy.

Now we both got brothers 'n both got sisters,
'n both of us know some misses 'n misters,
but fer reg'lar times ('r needin' favors),
we git that look 'n ring up the neighbors.

Y'see, git-a-long neighbors are a godly gift;
they soothe the soul in a world 'o rift.
'N as the years pass 'n they're tried 'n true,
they're jist the right spice fer me 'n you.

'Cause we all kin have a lotta things
'n fill our days from spring to spring,
but mostly we should learn ta savor
those gifts 'o time from darn good neighbors.

So when you're needin' a reg'lar time
'r if'n you feel tha' sun don't shine,
stretch yer days … make 'em slower,
jist call t'the neighbors … 'n have 'em over.

Raising Days

There's something about big red barns
more soothing than other shelters...

These farm monuments conjure scenes
of Raising Day
where a few dozen men in white shirts gathered
with women in long dresses and bonnets
and children playing 'crack the whip'
like in Homer's painting.
Neighbors were neighbors back then.

The two foot thick foundation
took some years of rock picking
from fields draft horses plowed with a single shear
for hand planted row crops.
Sand was hauled from the river
mixed with lime from the marsh for mortar.
The footings were deep shovel dug and rubble poured,
the sturdy walls quilted onto the footings
straight as a string,
the stones' flat side facing in ...
The rocked livestock parlor eight feet high
so horses would hit their heads if they reared.

The posts and beams usually were from tall oaks
felled with a cross-cut saw, trimmed
and broadaxed or sawed into ten by tens
then hewn with an adze.
Mortise and tenon joints were fashioned
between the corner posts, the bents

and the sill plates, cross beams, purlins, joists,
    and angle braces
were locked with whittled tapered pegs
pounded in holes drilled by an awl.
All this work ... the endless effort
made everyone strong.

The upcoming Raising Day was exciting for the family
who often lived in a temporary sod house near a spring.
They survived the years
erecting the foundation and the barn framing
by women tending gardens,
canning vegetables, storing fruit, potatoes, and squash
    in the root cellar.
The men rifled or trapped game and caught fish
precious grains were stored in barrels or hanging bags,
stone milled for baking, piecemeal.
The granary would come later.
Firewood was bow-sawed or chopped for tough winters.

Belled cows roamed the meadow,
horses were tethered close,
chickens, geese, ducks and guineas scurried about,
there was a dog or two hanging around, maybe a cat.
When the weather felt fair for several days and all was ready,
the neighbors came with heaping baskets of hearty food.

Raising Day began
by hoisting one ground assembled skeleton end,
poled upright, secured plumb and level,
the horizontal beams joined to inner upright bents,
the other end eventually hoisted, the joints all pinned
the sideboards, roof boards and the mow floor

hard hammered with smithed square nails.
The froe-split shingled roof laid,
a perfect size cupola for ventilation,
several weeks of painting iron oxide color
highlighted the elegant structures'
simple inviting lines.

The barn square dance with a caller and his fiddlers
went late into the night ...

Cattle and horses, maybe a few pigs moved in ... sheltered,
scythed hay was dried,
pitched onto a wagon
and loose stacked in the mow to winter the stock.

Barns store chaptered history of life
when neighbors were neighbors
and the country was young.

Grandpa's Anvil

I have my Grandpa's sturdy anvil
I watched him grip the hammer handle
and raise it high and strike a blow
to bend the iron in red hot glow

to keep his horses in perfect shod.
They'd pull in step, their heads a' bob
in collared harness they'd break the sod.
On Sunday's rest, he'd pray to God.

He tended crops with muscled hands
on blackened soil ...deep glaciered land.
I think of Grandpa's hardened times
his bygone rhythm, smithing chimes.

I see him strike his anvil still
his soul was strong ... from tempered will,
I hear his voice ... the words he said,
"take my anvil ... forge ahead."

Part
3

Sandhills

There's nothing quite like those Sandhill cranes.
No other bird is really the same,
high in the sky on outstretched cruise,
back on land they seem to muse.

I hear them coming a mile away,
that squawk-chatter thing they always say,
They're just majestic in soaring flight,
my favorite, though, is their alight
when they set their wings and sink straight down,
extend long legs and land aground.

Funny thing, though, about these cranes,
in mating season, they go insane,
the things they do with love on the brain.
They shriek and scream and jump around,
soon there they are … two eggs aground.
Cranes give comfort to me and you
I love those cranes and Ed does too.

*Ed Minihan is our long-time town chairman who made the
Sandhill the Town of Dunn symbol.*

The Father in Me

I saw my Father the other day
standing there just smiling,
like he did when I was a kid.
I recall he never spoke to me directly
but I remember how he was,
bustling around our hardscrabble farm
trying to forget the thirties' depression,
raising more food than we could eat.
He taught me how to work,
he rarely took time to play.
He didn't give me everything I wanted
(like a pony, Billy the neighbor had).
I learned to fix and make things on my own
as he was gone a good deal
helping other farmers decide
when their stock was ready for market
or delivering his farm report on the radio every day.
I learned to be kind though
since he never said a harsh word about anyone.
I learned to be humble
As he never bragged about himself.
I learned to be honest
on the day he returned a small pack of gum
I'd snitched into a grocery bag when I was four.
I'm sure he struggled
since his dad died at forty six
from a hard horse-kick to his flank.
Somehow, I never really felt fathered growing up back then
but I do now.

I walked over to him
reaching for his roughened hands
and was going to say
"Thanks for everything, Dad."
I wanted to mention
the gumption he gave us all
and how proud I am to be his son,

but I woke up and started my day,
thinking of my father in me …
more aware he'd given me everything I needed
before he died a few decades ago.

'Ol Hick'ry

In the middle of our field
on the the rolling ground
there's a big ol' hickr'y standing proud
that all before have plowed around.

Born centuries ago
yet watching me
he haunts me some
that majestic big 'ol hickr'y tree.

So I always walk over just to see
as he thrives upon the prairie sea
his giant leaves, the last to show
his patience wise
as he slowly grows.

I touch his orchids, his velvet brand
and wait for the nuts
he'll hide 'n his hands.
I lean upon his stalwart trunk
to feel his strength.

From years he marks
he's fifty feet wide, a hundred feet tall
he boasts orange leaves
in approach of fall,
then I search for his seeds
and bury them all.

I'm never alone by that lofty tree
for he somehow always comforts me...
I become lost in time
by this friend of mine,
that sturdy big 'ol hick'ry tree.

The Night Marauder

Did you hear that hoot of the Great Horned Owl?
I figure he's prob'ly on the prowl
for meals he hungers … mammals and fowl
he spooks me some … that big ol' owl.

With fierce yellow eyes he sees straight through
the blackened night that me and you
are blinded by when moon is slivered
his deep dark hoot … it makes me shiver.

I've seen him fly only now and then
from where he lives in nearby glen,
when off he goes to hunt the night …
the critters cringe when he takes a-flight.

A swift dispatch and then they're gone …
he flies them off with steely brawn
and hauls them up to branch 'fore dawn
to pick them clean, their gullets drawn.

He's quite the stealthy stalking machine,
a wise strong bird that's rarely seen,
his menu's long, his list of slaughter,
I like him though… this night marauder.

He dines on primes of his delight,
then disappears before it's light,
yet we know he's there, preying at night
in a world he reigns beyond our sight.

Kingfisher

I just heard that kingfisher clatter,
a false alarm of something-the-matter.
He hangs around our streams and ponds
though he'll take a snoop to woods beyond.

So now I'm duly focused on
where he lights and where fish spawn
I love to watch him perch on branch,
then cock his head with ready stance
and give the wary fish a glance.

Then he'll hover some and dive full force
piercing the water to spear his course
of tasty minnows he loves to sport.

Then out he splashes to quickly rest
as water beads off his belted breast,
his loopy flight so full of zest
as he chatters toward his tunnel nest.

The water slicks his ducktail head
a pointed arrow that fishes dread
yet his legs can't walk, a tad absurd
for such a handsome, happy, funny bird.

The Big Burr Oak

All of us have a favorite tree,
ours the neighbors big burr oak
just down the road a piece.

She's perfect round … one limb hangs down …
with massive trunk she stands alone.

She drapes on over …
a comfort tunnel … across the rustic road.
For years and years it caught our eye,
and gave us strength while passing by.

There's reds and blacks as well as whites
but hearts go out to big burr oaks
who wrestle hard in natures' fight
to catch some rays of nourished light.

They're gnarled and twisted, they're gristly, they're
tough
their branches look prickly, though smooth, not rough.
come wintertime … we glance up high
and watch their bony fingers … touch the moonlit sky.

Some years ago, a drifting car, crashed our favorite tree
and changes came once again upon the prairie sea.
We prayed to god …

She tried so hard … to grow and stay alive,
but we knew some day…
she would lay … and slowly might she die.

I think of centuries she thrived and grew,
struggling droughts and storms that blew,
her acorns shed … for forests new.

The last few years we all could tell
more naked limbs had cast a spell
as seasons passed … she wasn't well.

When I heard she must come down.
I shall not hear her crashing crown
I won't be there … can't bear to see
the felling of this glorious tree.

But then I noticed a stick of life … on the prairie sown
a young burr sapling sprouting there … right next this
    dying oak.
I stare into time … at his bark, his cloak,
I love what will become … of that baby burr'ed oak.

Barn Swallows

I finally saw a swallow scout!
I'z just wonderin' his whereabouts!
But now he's back to tell the others
it's time to return where they were mothered.

They've been gone to hinterland
since no bugs here in winterland,
uncanny they come right back to our barns
so happy they seem on tiny farms.

Swallows are such stunning flyers
with sharpened wings, the kings of gliders …
they dart and turn and swoop and swing
graceful cruisers … wing to wing.

I pause awhile to watch each day
proud they're here and proud they stay,
now I leave shed doors ajar
I hardly care if they white my car.

Swallows … the best of acrobats
thank god they are for there are cats
who lurk around on hunger track
for birds are tasty, we all know that.

They seem such perfect flying machines
they're just so sleek, yet rarely preen
their soft brown necks and shined blue wings,
an aerial show for us in spring.

The best thing, though, is how they snatch
those darn mosquitos and all the gnats

so we can work or eat outside,
so nice for us than stuck inside.

I spy their perfect pointed tails
they use to swerve and bank and sail,
they fly so high … then dive toward ground
they're up … they're down … they're all around.

If I pass too close to their mudded nest,
they surprise attack like I'm some pest,
they dive my head and I feel air rush
right through my hair, a warning brush.

I wonder why they rarely rest
but soon I see gaped mouths in nests
who quickly grow and soon to fledge
in fall they'll leave … a day I dread.

Then all at once they do take rest …
and I think to myself …
I guess they left.
No! Here they come! The squadron of swallows
who fly so fast my eyes can't follow.

As summer wanes I know they'll go,
one day I'll awake… no swallow show.
They'll be on their way, this merry band
to a southern place … their winterland.

So I'll wait till spring for they'll be back …
the best of pleasure to count on that,
thinking of swallows just comforts me
and the day they're gone … they're all I see …

Drought

We're having a drought,
no doubt about
no rain, all shine
we're pickle in brine.

Stunned by dry …
No reason why …
Seems the worst …
Our world in thirst.

Everyone sad …
Have we been bad?

Droughts sprout fear.
Eyes sprout tears
for crops now parched,
yet onward we march.

Dust from drought …

We're 'bout to shout
For clouds to come by
and fill blue sky.

No use to pray
for wilted hay.
Soon rain will stay …
We'll forget these days.

Sweet Dreams

I have dreams as we all do
where I'm gliding on a magic carpet
just like in that movie ...
and it seems so perfectly real
until I wake up right before I crash.

I have dreams where
people from decades ago pop up
and we're all having a good time ...
or a weird time ... somewhere ...
sometimes in a very strange place.

I have breathless dreams
where I can't keep up at work
racing from one gurney to another
and the patients have to wait
longer than they should
though no one died as I remember.

I have dreams I am back on the farm where I grew up
or sometimes on my own farm ...
sometimes an odd blend of both ...
my parents occasionally make guest appearances
though they died twenty years ago
they never talk to me in my dreams ...
(just like when I was a kid)
they are just there ... being with me.

I have dreams where bears
are stalking me
or sometimes herds of buffalo
are stampeding all around
as I cling to a small tree on the prairie.

I have dreams I'm spinning on a merry-go-round
laughing and dizzy but I can't get off
I have dreams I'm on a roller coaster
where I'm holding on for dear life
but the ride come to an abrupt stop
as I open my eyes, walk to the kitchen,
realizing they were all just dreams.

I have comfort dreams too
since I'm in love with you
caressing your back
as we fall asleep
then wake up happy like we do
the sweetest dreams are made of you.

Good News

The farmer's almanac says it's to be a long cold winter again,
just like last year when we had snow cover for six months
the worst winter in one hundred years,
the temperature often twenty below,
that north wind would freeze your face if you weren't careful.
Ice kept blanketing everything and many folks slipped and fell.
Last winter was cruel to the birds and even the furry critters.

I tried not to shudder about the upcoming winter.
I prefer to think about good news in the forecast
perhaps we'll get together with friends and family a little
    more often.
Maybe take in a few more good movies.
Maybe go for a sleigh ride or two.

Winter makes me think of spring
and that's the best news for spring always shows ...
I can picture the first crocus,
then the rhubarb
followed by April asparagus.
The birds will be back ... singing their hearts out
I'll start planning my favorite thing of all ... May morel
    mushroom hunts.
I'll till the garden for sweet corn and tomatoes
and dream of a bacon, lettuce, tomato sandwich with red
    onion and mayo
which is without a doubt (and no arguing here) the best
    sandwich on the earth.

Every year thoughts of spring help us handle fierce blizzards of winter.

Besides, my wife and I got a puppy in October, so we're all set no matter what.

Winter Wheat

In fall
the greening wheat
contrasts the harvest corn,

and soon the sprouting shoots
will brace for winter storms.

For then comes snow,
its blanket froze
the freshly planted ground,
but winter wheat
can always sleep
within the bitter cold.

When March comes 'round
their roots still bound
deep in warming soil,
a welcome sight
in brighter skies
for sleepy wintered eyes
is greening wheat …
in stalwart stand
amongst the other resting land.

The next few months,
the springing wheat
will turn a lighter green
with spindling straw
and budding heads
That hold the precious seeds.

Then in July,
the golden wheat
contrasts the greening corn …
The wavy fields of ripened grain
make busy days ahead …
when sheaves of wheat
are soon in store
to bake our daily bread.

Buzzards

Buzzards are old or so they say,
yet there they are on most our days,
they glide and glide ... and hardly flap,
they're hard to watch, they live on scraps.

Red wrinkled heads ... no beauty here,
but nature's way when death is near.

I spy a single way up high,
then moments later the flock arrives,
they lazy float ... then circle deeper,
this silent band of black Grim Reapers.

Winter Wood

On a cool fall day
my brother and I push and pull
the worn wooden handles of our six foot cross-cut saw,
slicing the thick trunk of a standing dead oak
that thrived for over four centuries
before it slowly died some years ago.

Our rhythmic labor is exciting
as sawdust slowly covers our boots
for we remember that year
a while back
when winter stretched into May
and our woodpiles had long disappeared to garden ash.
We'd hitch the team and roam the forest
for deadfall scraps
to warm our families
and cook hot food instead of smoked meat and fish
and vegetables and fruits from a canned jar.

Never again we said …
Now we're years ahead …
We smile as we bucksaw logs to chunks
we wallop with wedges and finish split with a double-bladed axe
piling them high in the woodshed.

We rest now and then
to admire the stacks …
filled with solid comfort
making Winters' Wood.

Flowing Waters

I'm always drawn to flowing waters
a silent strength that lures me farther …

I walk the carved and twisted paths
some before have also passed …

I feel the breeze that flutter leaves
of cottonwood and willow trees

I hear the babbling rippled churning,
the water on its endless journey …

Buoyed by springs clear and steady
I wade the constant swirling eddies …

And feel the current powering past
roiling up the silted sands …

I board a raft I leave untied
to see where shifting secrets lie …

Soon floating free in drifting sleep
from gentle rapids rhythm beat …

I dream of deltas dead ahead …
born within this rivers' bed …
In twilight slumber, far from home
slipping into worlds unknown.

On quiet current … gliding farther
around the bends of flowing waters …

Snowtrap

Great relief that January thaw
when snow became slush,
though I heard an elder say
"Beware the Snowtrap."

Winter blasted back with fury,
turning the half melt
to disturbing icestone,
our landscape now unwalkable
even for dogs.

Snow blown from the north
in the darkness and covered light.
The quiet morning sunny and still,
our white world becalmed
in silent apparition ...

Gravity strikes the unaware,
ankles and wrists and hips and heads,
changing lives, some sent
to their abrupt funeral.

Days of alarm ...
ice cleats, baby steps,
beware the pretty view,
A snowtrap lurks beneath ...

Lighthouse Keeper

I often dream I'm a lighthouse keeper
just me and the wavy sea.
I'll forever mark the waters deeper
for ships to pass upon the lee.

When the fog turns thick and creeps about,
they'll always see my lighthouse shout …

"Steer clear the shoals!
Don't run aground!
for Davy Jones,
he's lurking 'round …
amidst his pile of bones."

I'll never have a lonely hour
with the wind and the changing skies
where reds turn blue and blues turn gray
that misty time at the end of day.

Forget-us-not … the lighthouse keepers
for passing ships in the dark of night.
We always mark the waters deeper
and keep our beacons burning bright!

I love to dream I'm a lighthouse keeper,
it's where I want to be
to safely guide a sailor's course,
just me and the crashing sea.

Henry's Ghost

There is a ghost within our house
that we can hardly talk about,
we keep his candle burning still
on hallowed shrine, his honored will.
'Ol Henry's ashes in his urn,
his empty collar makes us yearn
for that loyal friend of my dear wife
who soothed her soul with all his life.
I hear him pad on down the hall
past his portraits on the wall,
when he couldn't walk we began to pray,
our toughest day when he had to lay,
those deep dark eyes that never lied,
we cried so hard the day he died.
A special dog we love so dear,
we live our lives just like he's here.

Maine

I often dream of coasts in Maine
the 'scapes that Homer loved to paint,
where lonely seas crash rocky shores,
where winds are strong and sea gulls soar.
The hardy few who chose to live
by fertile waters with life that gives
a deeper strength most never have,
these sturdy souls in rugged land.
I have a yearning for coasts of Maine
whose beauty reigns beyond the plains.
I must return and live some days
in sculptured lands on shores of Maine.

Iceland

You can tell right off Iceland is hard scrabble
with only a few wild reindeer about
and ravens on rooftops lurking for scraps.
In the treeless countryside the barns are half buried,
some farmsteads have an empty small steepled church
just for the family it seems,
maybe a neighbor comes for Sunday worship.
They say a volcano explodes now and then
amid the glaciers and rivers
making more waterfalls and geysers.
Ponies are everywhere, heads hanging down,
staring at the moss.
I'm floating in a hot springs lagoon
with my hair frozen hard
glancing at the northern lights
thinking about the arctic circle
and the good fresh cod,
wondering how many would live here
if the heat wasn't free,
wondering if I will have time left to return ...
to Iceland.

Theresa

If you ask me about beauty
I have to think for a while ...

Maybe someone dancing
a flawless ballet performance
Some striking stone architecture ...
a museumed oil painting ...
Some literature line, poetry perhaps,
a pure voice singing Ave Maria ...

But too, a rose blossom, a lady slipper, an orchid,
a grand old oak perched on a hill in a prairie,
a rushing stream in a true wilderness ...
the sky full of sunrise or sunset ...

Mostly, though, it's the smile in your eyes
when you look into mine ...
and we know we love each other.

Facing East

I've been awake for awhile,
Facing east in the morning twilight,
sitting on the edge of Lake Michigan
with the occasional lap of a wave
against the ancient rock beach …
Small flocks of ducks hurrying just above the water,
a quiet gull searching … gliding.

I wait …
Then crimson fire shoots
from the top of his head,
as he peeks across the lake … staring at us all …
We're face to face …
He could burn your eyes I've heard.
Slow and gentle, he comes up …
and gradually turns yellow … and warm.

I head back,
lie down for a bit and read,
wondering who else watched him.

Facing east when he's through,
dining on the beach with rhythm waves
in reddened sky surround
Soon too dark to keep reading,
with stars there as they should
a few flame out, streaking somewhere.

I'm ready, waiting …
in a time suspend …
until a small glow arrives … always in the east.
His enormous bald white head peeks over the water
lighting the night …
The moonbeam stretches seven miles across the
shimmering water …
Slowly … his face is full,
that same perfectly round face with that odd friendly
mouth.

He dims the stars some
and I can read again if I turn around
holding my book
to the side of my shadow.

Part
4

Sip of Gin

It's dusk
I've been reading a book off and on
and thinking about how I let some good friends slip away
when they sailed down a different river.

I happen to glance at my 'to do' lists on the side table
resting next to my chair, forever handy.
I spot my 'master' list of all the other hurried lists
shuffle through them, deadline a few items I finished today.

I recall laughing last night with the neighbors
about my groundhogs who keep digging holes under the fence,
eating my low hanging tomatoes in either twilight,
ruined the very day they ripen.

Tomatoes bring up my mother
who impossibly kept the cellar stocked
with canned peaches, pears, tomatoes, grape juice, pickles,
feeding six every day mostly from the garden.

I look over at the fire,
stare at worn out snoring ol' Buster ...
I figure I'll know the dreaded day
but he and I have today
just like we all do.

The book loses its grip
so I mark my place
struggle a bit to rise
and straighten

not quite tall
as I once was ...

I have a medicinal sip of gin,
go around the corner,
hang my jeans and Stormy Kromer
on the hall-tree
and lie down
in days-end great pleasure
next to my wife
drifting asleep on her side
in the afterdusk.

The Window

When I was young
I passed by a window slightly ajar,
barely giving it a glance
since the panes were foggy, the view to the inside hazy.
I didn't even break stride as I recall
staying the course on my narrow path of hurry.

Lately, I have become intrigued by that window,
I often dream about what was in there …
so I have decided to keep an eye out for it.
The allure, the excitement is overwhelming
to see if it is still open
and could it take me to where it might have
back then
since I know now where it could've.

It took quite some time
before I stumbled upon it.
There it was up ahead.
I picked up my pace.
The window came into clear view.
Indeed it was the very same one!
The search was over.

Alas, it was boarded up
shuttered tight by time …
I stood there staring at it
for a minute or so
reflecting on the past
yet at my age I wasted no remorse,

quickly promising to open the next window
of Chance.

I will at least stop
peek inside
take a hard look around
to see if the view is better through that window
than the one I am peering out now.

Slow 'er on Down

Every day I say I'll slow 'er on down,
for it seems we're always at Churchill Downs
where we prance to our slot in the starting gate ...
then bolt through time to never be late.

We gallop 'n we race towards the finish line
with made up reasons in passing our time.
so off we go to forget our fears
and then they're gone ... those runnin' years.

We don't really talk or look in our eyes
with so many people just livin' their lives
while charging on through till the day they die ...
never seeming to pause or figure just why.

So me, I promise to savor my days
for soon it's over in too many ways
I vow to do it, I surely say

I'll smell some red clover
which bees turn over
into honey ...

Which I'll spread
on my bread ...
for the morning race
at the starting gate.

Shelves

I seem to be surrounded by shelves.
I have several bookshelves for the read and the unread,
bric-a-brac shelves for ... well ... bric-a-brac,
garage shelves stacked with equipment for everything,
basement shelves with whatevers waiting for the ride to Goodwill.
The most useful, certainly, are kitchen shelves, hiding behind
   cupboard doors
so the clutter won't appear distressing.

I do have some very sturdy shelves where I put people ...
like the ones who've come over and blabbed only of themselves.
Some likeable folks are on there also, perhaps just forgotten
or maybe I'm sitting on a people shelf over at their place for
   some reason.
I just decided (now that I am looking at my people shelf) to
   build a big door for it
so the murmuring will stop.

In the attic, I have a large mistake shelf
but the additions seem smaller these days.

In my head, I have priority shelves somewhere in my amygdala
that I'm always rearranging, front to back mostly,
which makes me feel on top of things
until I come across forgotten 'to do' items
like building extra bathroom shelves for my wife's burgeoning
   grooming supplies
and petting the dog a little more.

The Closet

Like we all do
I have a closet somewhere in the attic
where I throw things no one would ever guess I own
like those years I smoked cigarettes
and that Quaalude I ate once in college
along with times I saddened a few gals
when I led them on for a while before I dulled them off.
(Though I never told them I loved them or anything.)
The key to my secret closet is inside my sleeping pillow.

Hidden in a far corner of my closet are some extra painful
    items …
Some endearing friends I lost track of,
and those times I should've told my parents
how much I loved them before they died.

In another corner there is a tiny pile of gold …
valuable lessons I learned myself about myself
like those years I kept trudging up the wrong way
of a one way street, blind to the red warning signs, until I was
    almost
killed by a horde of traffic that clearly had the right of way.

Sometimes as I drift to sleep on my pillow
I think of cleaning out the junk in my closet
but it seems much of it is decaying nicely on its own,
buried by dust and the happy trail I'm traveling now.
Besides at my age
I am too tired to poke around in my attic with some curious
    psychiatrist …
My third wife just gave me a new pillow anyway.

Gone Girl

It's been a fun few days
though I'm a bit weary,
the amusement worn off some
from doing naughty things I do
when my wife leaves to work for a bit or visit her family.

I start by feeding our mastiff Silvie scraps out of my hand,
lying down whenever I feel up to it,
watching Missouri Breaks, a little known but terrific Western
   movie
with Jack Nicholson, Marlon Brando, and Randy Quaid,
I follow that by staring at the golf channel for tips
while gorging on Frosted Flakes I just bought,
M & M's and caramel corn.

I should be doing fix up jobs around here
but I don't feel like it this February,
I don't wipe down the kitchen island countertop
until right before she comes back anyway.
I often walk around naked at the end of the day if it's warm
   enough,
and I sometimes don't lift up the lid on the toilet
but if I do miss, I clean.

I go to bed whenever I want
and I plan on sleeping in
since it is too cold to let the chickens out,
but actually I can't sleep nights
because Silvie snores louder than normal
while she dreams and runs in place
as we spoon each other all night.

Always on Sunday

Back in the fifties I'd get dressed up
in a little sport coat and pants that were either too big
(so I could grow into them)
or too small when the white shirt cuffs stuck out beyond my
coat sleeves.

This was Sunday and Mom would be putting on makeup
sitting at her dressing table in her slip,
Dad shaving standing at the poorly lighted sink mirror,
all six of us silently getting ready to
'Go to Church.'

We kids hadn't a choice.
An unspoken rule for that day.
Everyone in small Midwestern towns went to some sort of
church back then
unless you were a family of 'hoods' or something
though there were plenty of crooks and wolves in sheep's
clothing in the front rows.

Our family hardly ever missed (since we never took vacations
from the farm)
except a few times when my brother ran off and hid somewhere
but of course Mom would forgive him
as forgiving is the foundation of the Christian deal.

Mom would sing her heart out during the hymns,
always a touch off key but no one cared really
as we were all busy standing up or sitting down
and Dad would give the odd guest sermon
which is about the only time he ever preached to me.

I quit 'Going to Church' as soon as I got to college
since I found that God didn't punish me
for doing some real naughty things,
like drinking beer and trying to get laid with some co-ed
I didn't even know.

Along the way I figured out that
Jesus was likely a good person and all
but there is no way he came back
from being speared to death three days prior
moving that boulder by himself, I mean 'come on'.

Yet I do understand most all religious faiths
help people in times of trouble, offering hope
particularly when they are in some type of pain or perhaps
    dying,
but there is absolutely no scientific evidence at all
of a heaven or a hell.

Everlasting life I figure is when someone
has been influenced by you
in some form, be it genes or something you may have
said to them along the way
then they carry that part of you with them the rest of
their lives and so on.

We are upright mammals, known as the 'smartest
critters' but really the dumbest
as we are well on our way to ruining this incredible Earth
formed by the greatest explosion ever exactly 4.54 billion
years ago (give or take)
not created in seven days by god as the Old Testament purports
(with Sunday the day of rest).

Nowadays, many decades later, always on Sunday
I watch the CBS 'Sunday Morning' show for ninety minutes
(about the same length as a service)
while I'm eating the best homemade breakfast of the week
then leaf through the newspaper, turn on some Bill Evans,
Rarely thinking of
'Going To Church'.

The Party

I was sleeping the other night
and found myself at a gala party
with everyone bustling around
blabbing this and that.
I became engulfed with
couples coming up to me
and for some reason
they all thought I was interesting and funny.

I started to feel somewhat special
though I don't recall
what I was talking about.
I wondered why I was so popular.

Then I looked across the crowd
and caught a glimpse of my brother talking to a cluster of his
friends.
I realized he must have told them all
who I was or am.

Overcome by such a pleasant feeling
amongst all these folks
I didn't even know
was very comforting and totally unexpected.

The party went on for
quite a while ...
meeting lots of new folks,
a few stray women sidled up ...

But just as one was sizing me up pretty hard,
I woke for a bathroom break.

and the warm feeling from the partiers disappeared.

Settling back to sleep
I tried as hard as I could
to rejoin the party
but it was over ...
(yet I could hear some stragglers behind a door
somewhere in my hippocampus)

Anyway, I'll always remember the best party I ever
attended.

I hope he has another one some night soon.

Time

I wish I had more time
to try and figure just why
I can't seem to slow what time I'm left
for wasted days are nearly theft.

I try a slow and measured pace,
but it seems I live life's racing race
to go to places we're not sure where
and when we finish ... we're standing there.

Tomorrow! Tomorrow! I promise myself
I'll read those books upon my shelf,
and I'll be with all my dearest friends
with sweetened time that now I tend.

The River

Who are we then
that come upon a river
and watch the water glide
and stare deep in the current,
the current of flowing time.

We board a sturdy raft,
a raft to the unknown sea,
to search for what's beyond
and wonder where we'll be.
We sail upon the river,
floating free on a wand'ring stream,
we're guided by the channel,
passing shores of a settler's dream.
Who are we then, in wanderlust
heading towards the sea,
powered by the current
on water we used to breathe.
We sail through rippled churning
and watch the banks pass by,
aware of time that's turning
and stare upon the sky.
So soon our journey's ending,
so soon we have arrived.
We blend into the ocean,
to a sea where there is no time.

About the Author

John Herm was raised on a farm in Illinois before moving to Wisconsin to attend medical school. He'd always wanted to be a doctor and had a 41-year career as a noted Emergency Room physician. He started his poetry career decades ago with old-fashioned 'rhymers' about seeing the world of nature through the eyes of a young farm boy.

He still writes in his original style but these days also likes prose poetry. His idols are the late Eugene Field and Robert Frost, and the contemporary poet Billy Collins. In 2011, he was given a lifetime appointment as Poet Laureate of the Town of Dunn, a wonderful settlement near Madison, Wisconsin, dedicated to preserving greenspace and farms, which fits his style perfectly. His appointment has spurred him on to "write more poems than I ever imagined."

John divides his time between his Town of Dunn farm and his Washington Island cottage in Door County.

Acknowledgements

I would like to thank my father who recited Eugene Field's "Jest Fore Christmas" every year, my son Hunter for his photography, my wife Theresa and many friends and family for their encouragement, and Mari Anderson who kept after me to publish this book.
I would also like to thank the Town of Dunn for the Poet Laureate appointment.

43164052R00056

Made in the USA
Lexington, KY
30 June 2019